Mission, Strength, Potential: Keys to Strong Partnerships

Richard P. Swanson

ISBN: 979-8-218-19204-4

E-Book ISBN: 979-8-218-19205-1

DEDICATION

This book is dedicated to the memory of my father,
Ronald W. Swanson, a generous man.

TABLE OF CONTENTS

ACKNOWLEDGMENTS

I gratefully acknowledge the following reviewers of this manuscript for their thoughtful and critical comments. Any flaws or shortcomings of this book are my responsibility alone.

Michael Thomas Sunnarborg, author and consultant

If any of you have ever found yourself in the uncomfortable position of being suddenly terminated from your job, that makes you a member of what Michael calls the White Box Club. Michael truly wrote the book on how to cope with being fired, and how to move forward personally and professionally. Please read more about Michael and the White Box Club at:

https://michaelcreative.com/about/the-white-box-club/

Lori L. Jacobwith, founder, Ignited Fundraising

Lori is a master storyteller and consultant who helps nonprofit organizations tell their stories in compelling ways, which increases their ability to raise funds and donations. Please visit Lori at:

https://www.ignitedfundraising.com/

Christine Clifford, speaker, author, and business consultant

Christine is a vibrant and knowledgeable marketing and branding consultant and public speaker whose personal victory over cancer has inspired countless listeners. Christine has several books to her credit, including the recently released, "Let's Close a Deal". Please visit Christine at:

http://www.christineclifford.com/

I especially acknowledge my wife, Janet, who both tolerates and supports me through my failures and my successes. Her love and companionship sustain me more than I can express.

INTRODUCTION

Small business owners and nonprofit directors are among the hardest working people I know. They are passionate about their respective organizations, they are focused on success, they are persistent in the face of hardship, and they are generous with their time and expertise. When I think of the specific persons I know in these two roles, I'm reminded that they are people with whom I like to hang around.

The obstacles to success for small business owners and nonprofit directors are many. Financial resources are limited, and human resources are difficult to retain. It takes patience and a positivity to keep a smile on your face, and inspire others to smile with you.

Anyone who operates a small business or leads a nonprofit discovers that there is plenty of "how to" and "must do" advice to choose from, everything from creating your business plan to marketing your organization using social media, from how to get financing to the importance of creating your organization's brand. For multiple reasons and to varying degrees, most of this advice has merit. The tricky thing is to sort through, prioritize, modify, and sometimes reject the many pieces of advice you hear.

In my observation as both a small business owner and as president of small nonprofit organizations, nobody ever succeeds without the help of others. This reality flies in the face of conventional American wisdom and lore, where the heroes of our culture are rugged individualists whose singular leadership and perseverance result in massive success, wealth, and reputation. This book does not perpetuate that popular story.

This book is intended for the small business owner who has surpassed the magic three-year milestone (meaning, the business has survived into at least its third year), and created an entity that is successful as measured by these criteria:

The business generates enough net revenue to meet its regular monthly obligations, including employee salaries and overhead expenses;

The business has a customer base that is growing, no matter how modestly;

The business has a signature product or service that is its hallmark.

This book is also intended for the nonprofit director who leads an organization that is characterized by these measures of success:

The nonprofit maintains a list of donors and benefactors, and knows who has donated more than once;

The nonprofit has a volunteer base that is growing, no matter how modestly;

The nonprofit has stability in its officers or leadership roles (meaning, set terms, and no unplanned turnover or vacancies);

The nonprofit director and executive board have a strategic plan that is current and timely.

Additionally, this book is intended for the persons and organizations described above that seek the following:

A more widely spread positive reputation in their local community;

Greater access to human or physical resources than they have now;

Increasing numbers of customers or volunteers; Further protection against unforeseen risks faced by their business or organization.

I've developed an exercise by which small business owners and nonprofit directors strengthen their respective organizations through the relationships they build with each other. I've dubbed the exercise with the acronym SPARC, the letters of which I flesh out in detail in the chapters of this book. The book is motivated by my observations of working in the nonprofit arena since 1989, and by my recent experiences starting, operating, and consulting with small businesses since 2012. I see a missed opportunity for mutual benefit when small businesses and local nonprofit organizations build partnerships that put a SPARC into organizations.

I will also introduce you to the LIFE acronym that supplements SPARC and provides additional guidance as you create lasting professional relationships.

You will come to understand that central to forging these relationships are the key principles: **mission, strength, and potential.**

Let's go through the SPARC acronym together, so that you can waste no time seeking out new relationships that build your small business or nonprofit organization into the stable community resource you would like it to be.

1 SUSTAINABILITY

Sustainable giving inspires others

The traditional model of partnership between businesses and nonprofits looks something like this:

Company X has some surplus money sitting around, so the CEO of Company X finds Nonprofit Y and pledges $50,000 of support, which the Executive Director of Nonprofit Y promises to spend wisely, acknowledging Company X in its promotional literature. The Executive Director invites the CEO to attend their annual gala, at which the two shake hands and smile for the camera. Everybody feels good and goes home.

I am not intentionally mocking this scenario, and I do not belittle those who engage in either side of the relationship. A lot of good comes out of these exchanges that should not be overlooked or underappreciated.

The SPARC model does not teach or perpetuate this type of relationship, however, for several reasons:

The companies that can be philanthropic at this level or higher have money to burn, which eliminates most small businesses from following suit;

The nonprofits that can draw monetary contributions of this size or larger are of a size and reputation that far exceeds that of most nonprofits found in a community;

The relationship between donor and recipient can be fickle, and terminate suddenly without explanation.

It's my opinion that when a business donates money to a nonprofit, that is often the least they can do, even if they contribute significant sums of money. For small businesses, giving large sums of money is rarely sustainable. They try it for a year or two, decide there's no real payoff, and quit giving. Even large corporations change their mind from time to time. Here's an example I lived through.

Part of my career working in the nonprofit arena was spent at the local Public Broadcasting Service (PBS) affiliate in St. Paul, Minnesota, known then as Twin Cities Public Television (or "tpt" for short), and now called Twin Cities PBS. I had a very cool role as the Science Content Director for a children's science television series called DragonflyTV. Unlike other television production activity at tpt, our series was not funded by member pledges. Our show was funded by a combination of corporate sponsorships and federal funding. The series went into production in 2001, when a generous sponsorship from a local electronics retailer was secured.

The series launched successfully, the retailer was featured prominently in the opening and closing credits, and all was good for the first three years of the show's existence. At the conclusion of year three, the corporate sponsor withdrew further funding. They made it clear that it was not for lack of satisfaction with how we used their money, nor were they displeased with the television series or with having their name associated with our series. They simply said that they had other goals in mind, and DragonflyTV was not part of them. No malice, no hard feelings, but also no more money.

Happily for my co-workers and me, the television station found new funding sources, and DragonflyTV stayed in production for a total of seven seasons (a very long time as television shows go). The lesson I learned from this experience is that it's harder than it sounds to build a sustainable relationship between a business and a nonprofit.

As we work our way through the SPARC acronym, we are going to look at each letter from two sides: from the perspective of the small business, and from the perspective of the nonprofit organization. I will ask you, as either the small business owner or the nonprofit director, to remain attentive to both your role and that of your counterpart. We are not creating a simple donor-recipient relationship here. We are working toward a collaborator-supporter model in which both parties are working for the benefit of the other. This is a fundamental change, and I firmly believe this is how we build sustainable relationships between the two.

It's really out of the question for most small businesses to consider four-figure or five-figure charitable contributions. Even if a business could give $10,000, it could probably only do that once per year, and to only one organization. This requires the business to pick a favorite from among all nonprofits who are competing for contributions. Even when we scale down to three-figure contributions, it's going to be challenging to sustain this giving pattern.

I have four principles of sustainability for the small business owner to consider when it comes to charitable giving.

Sustainability Principle #1: Give within your means

This probably seems obvious enough, but I observe that well-intentioned small business owners often overshoot their capacity to give when first they venture into charitable giving. It's counterintuitive, but bigger is not always better. You might be surprised how much impact small contributions can make. Now, nonprofit organizations often structure tiered giving programs, meaning, the more you give, the more perks you get in return (more mentions in their social media output; more appearances of your company name and logo at their events; etc.) That's a bit of a trap, so I want you to watch out for that. There are other giving structures possible, and toward the end of this book I'll give you some ideas for how to negotiate them with a nonprofit partner.

And if you are a nonprofit director who is creating a tiered giving plan, I challenge you to think about alternative models. The tiered giving structure is well tested and well worn, but it doesn't work for all business partners.

The "give within your means" principle applies to more than just monetary contributions. I'll return to this in the chapter where I discuss the letter A of the SPARC acronym.

Sustainability Principle #2: Your contribution is something you are already doing

If you operate an established small business of at least three years of age, if your business is stable, and you have a signature product or service, then I want you to consider how to leverage what your business already does for the benefit of a nonprofit partner. This requires some creative and freethinking, and I have every confidence you'll immediately see the wisdom of this principle the first time you put it into practice.

Here's a quick example. I spent part of my career working for the Valspar Corporation (now owned by Sherwin-Williams) headquartered in Minneapolis,

Minnesota. Valspar has a longstanding charitable contribution program called "A Brush with Kindness", in which Valspar gives away house paint for free, especially to partners such as Habitat for Humanity. Seems like a no-brainer: Valspar makes paint, so Valspar gives paint away. During my time at Valspar, the company celebrated its millionth gallon of donated product… talk about sustainable!

The lesson for small business operators is clear: do what you are already doing well, and what you are making money at doing, and look for a way to leverage that for the benefit of a nonprofit partner. When you find what that activity is, chances are you can find a way to "give some away" without jeopardizing your primary revenue stream.

For the nonprofit director, the lesson for you is to think creatively about what sorts of contributions will benefit your organization and the people you serve. Money is always useful, but small business owners who are cash strapped may have something else to contribute, be it a product or a service or expertise, so be creative and open-minded about what you ask for.

Sustainability Principle #3: Your contribution generates a return

Some people will find this principle objectionable, so I'll have to make my case strongly. Let me state clearly for the record: Yes, in order for a small business to sustainably make charitable contributions it is right and proper to expect that there be some return.

The most challenging part of this principle is to determine how to measure the return, and to demonstrate the value of the return equals or surpasses the value of the contribution. If you contribute $500 to a nonprofit group, can you show that you earned back $500 worth of business from the nonprofit's client list who ultimately patronized your business? In most cases, the answer is, "Not very easily." Did Valspar sell a million gallons of paint to Habitat for Humanity volunteers who used Valspar's product while volunteering their time? Hard to say, but Valspar obviously determined it was worth it to them to donate that much product.

There's some tricky moral ground to navigate here, too. I don't think a small business can rightfully use their contribution to extort sales from their nonprofit partner's clientele. That's not what I mean by the sustainability principle of generating a return.

I learned a tough lesson from my tpt days on how large corporations sometimes view this principle. I mentioned already that our first corporate sponsor withdrew after the first three years of the series. We had a new corporate sponsor lined up, and they were nearly ready to commit to two years of sponsorship for our show. At the last minute, we learned they had withdrawn interest. Their leadership had calculated a projected return in the form of prospective viewership of their brand in the opening and closing credits. Based on the viewership history of our show, and projected viewership going forward, the leaders of the corporation felt it was more valuable for them to buy conventional advertising than to fund our series. Our series on public television couldn't compete with an ad buy on a commercial network during Saturday morning cartoons as far as "providing eyeballs" to our sponsor.

Sustainability Principle #4: Your contribution inspires others

I learned something about this principle when I participated in a fundraising "boot camp" while serving on the Advisory Board for Minnesota Collegiate DECA, a nonprofit group that supports informal business and entrepreneurship education at the collegiate level. Like so many nonprofits, Minnesota Collegiate DECA was struggling to maintain its donor base so that it could continue to provide basic educational services and events for its students. They turned to a fundraising consultant, Lori L. Jacobwith, who is founder of Ignited Fundraising.

Among the valuable lessons we all learned from Lori is the importance of telling your story in a compelling, emotionally powerful, and inspirational way.

The importance of this lesson is that small business owners and nonprofit directors have an opportunity to work together to tell an inspirational story. Experts like Lori L. Jacobwith can show you how to do this well. I won't pretend to provide that kind of expertise in this book. I will simply say that the most powerful examples of partnerships between businesses and nonprofits have inspirational stories to tell.

We're ready to look at the next letter of the SPARC acronym. I've hinted at it more than once already, so it's time to flesh it out in more detail. P is for Partnership.

2 PARTNERSHIP

Your Mission and Vision support your partnerships

When businesses and nonprofits engage in donor-recipient relationships they often miss the opportunity to be actual partners. Since the donor-recipient model is the least likely to work for small businesses and small nonprofits, I see it as vital to build a different model, which for me is a partnership model.

You may have recognized that SPARC does not assume there is a one-to-one exclusive pairing between a business and a nonprofit. These relationships are not marriages. Now, I am divorced and remarried, and for that reason you may think that I do not value marital fidelity. In fact, I do value fidelity and loyalty, and I have the utmost respect for couples that stay together once and for always. Businesses and nonprofits are not people, however, and I think the marriage analogy can only extend so far when applied to entities rather than people. While I don't believe "open relationships" are plausible for most individual persons, I'm a polygamist when it comes to business relationships. A business can be in a relationship with multiple nonprofits at once, and vice versa.

Now that I've laid that card out on the table, I'm going to quickly follow it with a second statement: Just because one business can enter into a relationship with multiple nonprofits doesn't mean it should. I have three principles that guide the decision about whether to pursue a partnership or not.

Partnership Principle #1: Mission and values of partners align

I hope that all readers find this principle to be the most valuable lesson they take away from this book. I think it's a great lens for viewing potential partnerships, and provides the strongest evidence for saying "Yes", and more importantly, for saying "No".

Developing a statement of mission and values is an exercise that most nonprofit organizations go through. I find that large corporations usually have a published mission statement, also, and often either a vision or a values statement. Small businesses either don't create them, or they don't publish them, and I think this is something all of us who start small businesses ought to spend some time doing.

When you, a small business owner, are looking for a nonprofit organization to support, I encourage you to spend time in discussion with your counterpart about their organization's mission and values. Of course, this means you have to be prepared to share your own. Your mission should be brief, memorable, even a little lofty, yet realistic, too. There are lots of consultants who will happily work with you to develop one. Large corporations may have mission statements that appeal to their stockholders, while their values statements appeal to their customers.

For the small business owner, think about a mission statement that would make your employees proud to say they work for you and inspire them to come to work each day, and a values statement that would make your customers pleased to buy your products and encourage their friends to do the same. You might even enlist the assistance of your nonprofit partner to provide you feedback on your statements as you craft them.

Let's fast-forward to the actual conversation between you and your potential partner. Let's imagine that both organizations have mission and values statements and you've shared them with each other. How do these statements help you decide whether or not to work together? Look for some characteristics you may have in common such as:

A common target demographic: the elderly; youth; athletes; artists; disabled; families; etc.;

A common purpose: education; empowerment; healing; recreation; wellness;

A common employee/volunteer demographic.

Further, there might be a more personal connection between the small business owner and the nonprofit director such as:

A shared personal interest: (nature preservation; support for veterans)

A common work history: (both are former teachers; both coach youth sports)

When these commonalities are found, they become discussion points for future collaboration. If you and your counterpart can't find something that binds you among these items, it's unlikely you will be motivated enough to develop a SPARC-like partnership. A donor-recipient relationship may still be possible, but you may not progress beyond that.

Partnership Principle #2: Define Roles for Both Partners

I find that strong partnerships have well-defined roles for all partners. Without this definition, tasks are uncompleted; assumptions lead to misunderstandings; dissatisfaction turns to frustration.

In a donor-recipient relationship, there is some inherent definition of role: I give you money; you spend it well. The best donor-recipient relationships provide further role definition about things such as promotional activity carried out by the recipient, or expectations for the donor's presence at the nonprofit gala.

When a deeper partnership is sought, it is necessary to be explicit about roles, responsibilities, and expectations. I like to use a tool I learned from my days as a quality improvement project manager to lay these roles out on the table. The tool is called a RACI matrix, where the letters of the acronym stand for Responsible, Accountable, Consulted, and Informed. In quality circles, the RACI Matrix is used to define roles and responsibilities for key players in a project team. I recommend using it to spell out how you and your partner will collaborate on a joint goal. Let's look at the matrix to see how it can be used.

The RACI Matrix is a grid with a listing of tasks or actions (responsibilities, in other words) shown down the leftmost column. Across the top one lists the titles of the individuals from both organizations that are the key players in these tasks. Here's an example that helps illustrate how to use the matrix.

Imagine the following tasks for a collaborative event with your organization and your partner:

Task list for collaborative event
Arrange venue logistics
Contact catering
Develop invitation language
Do set-up onsite prior to event
Send out invitations to nonprofit contact list
Send out invitations to small business contact list
Post event cleanup
Post event debrief meeting

Then, generate a list of roles, meaning, persons from both organizations, whom you would call upon to work on or oversee these tasks:

Nonprofit director
Small business owner
Nonprofit volunteer #1
Small business employee #1
Small business employee #2

Now you can create a matrix for the joint collaboration between a small business and a nonprofit in putting on a celebration honoring the nonprofit's volunteer base. Down the left column of a grid you put a high-level listing of tasks. Across the top you see the titles of persons from both organizations. A word about this: I find it preferable to list job functions here, rather than the personal names of specific individuals. You want the matrix to be applicable for the future. People change roles within their organization, or they leave altogether, so naming individuals in the RACI matrix can result in the matrix quickly becoming out-of-date or obsolete. Job functions are more stable and enduring, therefore, the matrix is likely to stand the test of time.

Now that the tasks are listed and the proper functions identified, it's time to fill in the grid. Rather than just using an X or a check mark, you use the letters of the RACI acronym as follows. For the first line item in the task list, identify which of the roles named will have primary responsibility (R) for carrying out the task. In the grid, place an R under the function. This is the task-doer. Secondly, consider who will be accountable (A) for ensuring the task-doer gets the work done on time. This is often the task-doers boss or manager. This individual has an A entered into the grid under their function title.

For any given horizontal line, there should at least one R and one A, and not more than one of each. Attempting to share either Responsibility or Accountability between two persons often results in confusion.

The remaining letters of the RACI acronym are C for consulted and I for informed. These are optional, yet helpful. Place a C under the function title for anyone to whom the Responsible individual may turn if they need guidance, insight, or authority when carrying out their assigned task. Place an I under the name of anyone who won't be carrying out the task, but ought to be made aware of progress on the task.

Here are some final guidelines for filling in the grid:

Every row has one A and one R, and not more than one of either
It is not necessary that each row have a C or an I; there can be more than one of either.
It is not necessary that each square of the grid be filled in with a letter.

Let's imagine how a grid like this could be filled in.

Consider the task "Arrange venue logistics". The person assigned to make the arrangements could be the Nonprofit Volunteer #1, designated with R. The Nonprofit director holds that person accountable for completing the task, as designated by the A. The Small business owner partner could be consulted as to the choice of venue, so a C goes in the grid there, and another employee from the small business will be informed of the goings on, designated with an I.

Partnership Principle #3: Meet regularly

In order to get the full benefit of the partnership it will be necessary to meet with your counterpart on a regular basis. I suggest meeting at least quarterly, and possibly monthly. These could be one-hour meetings over lunch, or conference calls, or even business golf outings if you both are willing to commit the time. The term "business golf" has a specific meaning for me, and I have a set of well-defined rules for how a round of business golf should be set up and played. In short, it is a round of golf played for the purpose of establishing trust, not for the purpose of brokering a deal or getting away from the office on a sunny day.

What do you discuss when you meet with your counterpart? You're building a lasting relationship between yourself and your counterpart, and between your respective organizations. In time, you'll find you have more than enough to discuss, and, in fact, you have more discussion items than will fit into the time you have allotted. Here is a short list:

Upcoming promotional events
Obstacles to success
Lessons learned from recent successes
Challenges with employee or volunteer recruitment/management
How to find and retain board members
Lessons learned from social media marketing campaigns
Changes in the business or fundraising climate, and how to plan for them.

You might say, "Well, these are things I would only discuss with trusted colleagues," and I would say, "Exactly!" Remember, as a small business owner, you aren't simply looking for someplace to spend your money; you are looking for someone who is interested in your success. For you as a nonprofit director, you aren't just looking for a financial contributor; you are looking for someone with expertise that you can leverage to the benefit of your organization.

I've developed a "SPARC a Conversation" Interview Tool that you can use as a guide for discussion with potential partners as you get to know each other and determine whether or not it will be beneficial to you both to work together. You can access the "SPARC a Conversation" Interview Tool by navigating to the website indicated in the Appendix, and you can download it from my website. Let's move on to our next letter of SPARC.

3 ASSETS

You have more assets available to you than you may realize.

When I operated my business consulting practice, I helped some of my clients look for additional revenue streams for their nonprofit organization. As part of that exploration, I led them through an exercise where I helped them identify all types of business assets they had available to them that had untapped potential for revenue. Together, we generated a list of more than 70 assets they had available. Next, we brainstormed ways the organization could leverage those assets to bring new income. Finally, we sorted and prioritized the brainstormed list, and identified two new strategies for implementation, each of which had the realistic goal of bringing in an additional $25,000 annually into the organization.

When most businesses think about their assets, they think of the obvious things: available cash; inventory and raw materials; human capital; equipment and facilities; patents and trademarks. Small businesses and nonprofits alike often consider themselves asset poor. In fact, they often have much more available to them than meets the eye.

In my first book, Success and Happiness from the Ashes, I tell the story of starting my first business, and feeling very much defeated by the reality that I was about to become part of the statistic that 75% of all small businesses fail within three years. There was, in fact, a success story that came out of that episode, namely, I put myself through the exercise of identifying the assets I had accumulated in less than three years time.

I firmly believe tapping into underutilized assets opens up a new conversation between small businesses and nonprofit organizations. In the traditional donor-recipient model, the currency of that relationship is money. In the SPARC model, businesses and nonprofits learn to trade in other currencies, namely, the untapped assets that each has but of which they may not be aware. Consider the following asset categories, with examples listed below them:

1) Operational Assets
a. Facilities and equipment
b. Social media presence
c. Marketing and brand collateral
d. Contact lists
e. Monetary assets
f. Public relations events

2) Service Assets
a. Services you provide to clients/customers already
b. Workshops
c. Classes
d. Webinars

3) Intellectual and Expertise Assets
a. Project management
b. Human resource management (recruitment; training; onboarding; talent development)
c. Office skills (word processing; spreadsheet skills; customer relationship management)
d. Process improvement (LEAN; Six Sigma; Agile)
e. Grant writing
f. Supply chain management

4) Hidden Assets
a. Employee/volunteer hobbies, pastimes, passions
b. Educational background of leaders

5) Human Assets
a. Key roles within your organization, and the people who fill them
b. StrengthsFinder™ attributes
c. Diversity and multi-generational attributes

6) Product Assets
a. Things you manufacture or sell
b. Patents or copyrighted material you own
c. Books, publications, white papers

There are over twenty categories in this short list already, and I barely scratched the surface. When you start filling in these categories with the specifics of your organization, you quickly have a list of over one hundred assets. And when you start a conversation with your counterpart, who also went through this exercise, now you have double that number of assets to work with and leverage on each other's behalf.

The beauty of this asset list is that it inspires creative thinking about what you can accomplish once you realize you have these assets available. We've broken through the traditional parameters established when money is the only currency available to you. Just think of the possibilities when you start trading in other currencies such as intellectual/expertise assets, human assets, or service assets.

Can you see how the conversation changes between a small business owner and a nonprofit director once you stop limiting yourself to discussions about money?

I have a quick reference guide on how to create an Assets Inventory that gives you and your counterpart some tips for discussing how to leverage assets other than money for your mutual benefit. You'll find a URL to the Assets Inventory Guide in the Appendix, so you can order it from my website. Let's look at the fourth letter in the SPARC acronym.

4 RELATIONSHIPS

Involve your employees and volunteers to build the strongest relationships.

At this point, I've likely given you the impression that SPARC is about building a relationship between two persons: the small business owner and the nonprofit director. If we stopped there, then I think we'd find a success rate of 50% at best. I want to raise the stakes and increase chances for successful collaboration. If we are going to do that, we have to get more people involved.

I want to return to the story I told you under Sustainability Principle #2 about Valspar's "A Brush with Kindness" program. I think the reason that it continues to be so successful is because it is more than an agreement between the CEO of Valspar and the top executive at Habitat for Humanity. Valspar properly recognizes that a key to success is to actively engage its employees at all levels in the program, and provide opportunities for its employees to take time to volunteer at Habitat for Humanity events. Valspar celebrates the participation of its employees in their local Habitat house projects, and encourages managers to assemble teams of employees to work en masse at an event. Employees always come back with a smile and a story to tell, and take more than a little pride in their own contribution, as well as knowing their employer supported these efforts.

I think this is a great lesson for small business owners who also want to build their reputation in the local community, and to increase employee engagement and satisfaction on the job.

Here are some principles for how to involve your employees and volunteers with your efforts at collaboration with your partner organization.

Relationships Principle #1: Serve side-by-side

The nonprofit partner has plenty of need for volunteers throughout the year, so structure an event where some number of the small business's employees gather together to work alongside each other and alongside volunteers from the nonprofit organization. Plan this strategically. The small business can't afford to shut down operations for a day in order to do volunteer work (this would be a bold move, however, and worthy of media attention!), so think small and think smart, and maybe send small groups of volunteers on several different weekends. Leadership by example is important here, so the head of the small business and her/his/their managers should include themselves in the mix. Mindfully encourage interaction between employees and volunteers, so that both leave with a sense of connectedness to the other.

Strive to hold service opportunities at least twice each year, and quarterly if at all possible.

Relationships Principle #2: Hold an Open House

There are numerous variations on how you can do this, and both partner organizations can take a turn.

A small business like a retailer can set up some sort of customer appreciation event for volunteers associated with the nonprofit partner. Be mindful, however, of using strategies such as discounting your products or services at an event like this. The point of holding an open house is to introduce new potential customers to your business and overwhelming them with your fabulous customer service. You want to leave them with a memory that naturally drives them to want to come back, and to tell your friends to shop your store, too. Win them over with great service, rather than discounts or pushy sales tactics.

Small companies that are not business-to-customer (so called B2C) but rather business-to-business (B2B) may take a different approach to holding an open house. If practical, a special behind-the-scenes tour of your facility for your nonprofit partner's volunteers, donors, and board members can make a very positive impression, and take advantage of the psychological phenomenon of allowing your guests to boast to their friends that they got to see something that not many people otherwise see.

Nonprofit organizations often have regular open house events; take advantage of those events to especially welcome employees and guests of your small business partner. Again, leave your guests with a positive experience and emotional connection to the good work your organization does every day.

Relationships Principle #3: Socialize

You want to get members from your two organizations interacting and making their own personal connections, so sometimes you just need to throw a party! Does your small business have an annual summer picnic? Consider opening it up to guests from your partner organization.

Look for a local winemaking club, and see if they will host a wine tasting event for your employees and your partner's volunteers.

Create other family fun events, such as attending your local minor league or semi-pro baseball team's home game. Hold a snowman-making contest. There are endless excuses you can make to bring people together for a smile and to create positive memories together. Remember to leverage those hidden assets you have lurking around your organization.

Relationships Principle #4: Engage the Third Partner

If you really want to make an impact and build a powerful relationship with your partner organization, then take an extra step to engage what I call the "Third Partner." I'll explain.

In business as in life, there are good relationships and bad ones. Think about the personal and professional relationships in your own life, and use the following descriptions to characterize them.

A. Lose-Lose

We've all had this relationship, and we've all struggled with either trying to change it or trying to end it. A lose-lose relationship is bad for you, bad for the other person, on lots of levels: emotionally, financially, and just about every other way.

B. Win-Lose

These relationships are just as bad, maybe even worse than Lose-Lose, because one party is coming out ahead and has reasons to try to keep the relationship as it is, even as the other party tries to get out. The risk of trying to improve the relationship is that it simply inverts to a Lose-Win.

C. Win-Win

This is the type of relationship we wish we always had in our personal lives and in our professional lives. These relationships don't just magically appear, and once you establish one, it requires care and feeding so it doesn't regress to a Win-Lose or Lose-Lose.

So that's all there is, right? I think there's one more relationship type that can be very rewarding, and it involves the Third Partner, namely, the group who stands to benefit when you and your collaborative partner extend your Win-Win scenario beyond yourselves…

D. Win-Win-Win

In some circles this is called the Triple Win scenario. By comparison, a standard Win-Win relationship is a closed loop between the two partners. Think of a simple seller-buyer relationship. This can turn out to be any one of the first three relationship types. If a seller sells a product at a severe discount to a customer who is dissatisfied with the product, both parties lose. If the seller sells the product at a severe discount and the customer is happy, it's a Lose-Win. If the seller makes a profit and the customer is happy with the purchase, it qualifies as a basic Win-Win. However, the relationship is closed, or contained, between the two parties.

Interesting things happen, however, when you re-structure a Win-Win scenario to add a third win for another party or group.

The real opportunity that small businesses and nonprofits have is to collaborate not only for their mutual benefit, but also for the benefit of an additional customer, group, or partner. Remember when I discussed Partnership Principle #3, and I encouraged you to meet with your counterpart at least quarterly, if not monthly, and you wondered what there was to talk about so frequently? You could spend all those meetings simply talking about Triple Win scenarios, and then bring them to life.

Who is the Third Partner? It may be the people served primarily by the nonprofit organization, such as disabled veterans, or low-income families with school age children. It may be a preferred charitable organization of one of your advisory board members. In general, the Third Partner is a person, group, or entity that benefits from the synergistic collaboration between you and your partner.

Let's get to the final letter of SPARC, where we "seal the deal" on our new partnership.

5 COMMITMENT

Your commitment will endure when you measure success.

Partnerships require commitment, so we ought to look at the nature of the commitment for the partnership I'm proposing that small business owners and nonprofit directors create together. Here are some concrete actions you can take.

Commitment Principle #1: Cross Promote

We've already talked about planning joint events like open houses and behind-the-scenes tours. Here, I'm suggesting that that you commit to promoting each other's events that aren't planned jointly. I'll assume that each of you has a presence on social media, such as Facebook, Twitter, Instagram, or LinkedIn. It does not take a lot of energy to develop and execute a simple social media campaign to promote your partner. Small businesses can engage their social media followers and highlight the good work that their nonprofit partner does each month. Nonprofit organizations can use their social media outlets to thank their small business partner for supporting their mission.

Commitment Principle #2: Create Reward Programs

Small businesses use referral programs all the time to encourage referrals from trusted partners. Referral groups like BNI (Business Network International) are popular with small business owners, and somewhat underutilized by nonprofit entities, which are sometimes frightened away by the annual membership fees.

There are lots of types of reward or referral programs you can set up, such as:

coupon codes
"frequent flyer" punch cards
referral points programs
rack cards

I know that some small business owners I have spoken
to will not engage in referral programs that are linked to
rewards. It feels more ethically clean to them to not
earn any perks for sending referrals to a trusted partner.
I respect that, even though I consider myself neutral on
the point. I think there are plenty of examples of
referral programs with rewards that are ethically
administered. The point is, this is one of the
conversations you have with your partner. Together,
you arrive at a program that is agreeable to both parties.

Commitment Principle #3: Donor or Customer Lists

I want to make a comment on leveraging your customer
list or your donor list. I think this is a particularly
slippery slope to traverse, so I have some thoughts to
share.

Whether you are a business or a nonprofit, you worked
hard to build up a list of email contacts who have
interest in your product or service, and who trust you to
respect the bond between you. I think it's unwise to
share lists or give your partner direct access to the
persons on your organization's list of contacts. I don't
recommend negotiating list access as part of your
agreement for collaboration. You may wish to acquaint

yourself with the CAN-SPAM Act of 2003, enacted by the Bush administration, for other guidance on proper and legal use of lists for email purposes. In the time since this book was first published, data privacy laws have strengthened, so don't run afoul of them.

I think it is appropriate to inform your potential partner of the size of your list as an indication of the scope of your organization's reach. I also think it is good to know some basic demographic data about the persons on your list. This knowledge may actually help you say, "No, I don't think we are a good fit for each other" and spare you both the unpleasantness of dissolving the collaboration later.

In short, your list of customers or donors belongs to you, and you should retain ownership of the list. In your regular communications to your list members, you can weave in news about your partnership with your counterpart, but the news should always come from you, not from your partner.

Commitment Principle #4: Measure Your Success

It's now a common truism in business circles that "what is measured is improved." Therefore, I think one way you show commitment to your partner is to commit to measuring the results of your collaborative work together. If you don't know the results of the work you do, you can't make a case for continuing the collaboration, or ending it, for that matter.

Knowing what to measure and how to measure it is a bit of an art form, and too many small businesses and nonprofits fail to track any measurements of performance at all. This is an avoidable mistake.

Meet with your partner, and discuss what performance metrics make sense, and how you will track them and report them to each other. Agree to evaluate the results of the data gathering at appropriate intervals, such as annually, semi-annually, or quarterly if warranted.

We've walked through the complete SPARC acronym together. I think you'll agree that this is not a variation of a "get rich quick" scheme. This model is a mindful and measured approach to building new partnerships. At the same time, I trust you have found principles that resonate with your own experience as a small business owner or nonprofit director. Moreover, I have biased my discussion towards the assumption that you will create one or more partnerships in the SPARC mold. But as always, the same tools that let you find a great partner are the same tools that allow you to decline working with a poor partner.

6 HERE'S TO LIFE!

Bring your partnerships to L-I-F-E

I have a few additional criteria for you to consider as you seek out potential partners and partnerships. I use the acronym LIFE to help you keep these criteria top of mind.

LIFE Principle #1: Laughter

As you get to know your potential partner and her/his/their organization, listen for clues that there is an element of laughter and joy in their organizational culture. Organizations whose members have reason to smile make great partners. Don't be shy about planning events with your partner that bring a smile to everyone's face.

LIFE Principle #2: Independence

In some ways, frankly, you are looking for a partner who doesn't need you. Maybe you don't really need them, either. That sounds odd, I know, but let me explain.

As you engage in conversations with potential partners, you want to establish yourself as coming from a position of strength, or what I consider to be independence. That is to say, you can honestly describe for your partner how your organization has weathered some storms, survived, and has evolved to a place where it is stable. That doesn't mean you don't have any needs at all… far from it. Rather, I think it is more appealing to a potential partner that they see that they are working with an organization that is not in dire straits.

I think we've all heard the pitch, "If we don't raise $10,000 by next month we'll have to cut programs and staff… won't you please help?" Sometimes, that's a true scenario, and the best response is simply a quick donation of cash. Again, that relationship is not what we are seeking with SPARC.

Show your potential partner the ways in which your organization is self-sufficient and independent. I think this a stronger posture than one in which you depend on another organization's support for your very survival.

LIFE Principle #3: Fit

Back in Chapter 2, I wrote about seeking alignment between your organization and that of your partner. Finding a business or nonprofit partner that "fits" you and your organization is a tricky thing. For example, is it obvious that a local sporting goods retailer could partner with a not-for-profit youth athletic league? Maybe that seems like a no-brainer, but I think there's a risk of a failed relationship if the two partners don't sit down, talk with each other, and really sort through what their respective and mutual goals are.

Remember, you don't have to dance with every wallflower at prom. Having a conversation with all of them doesn't hurt, however.

LIFE Principle #4: Energy

One of the characteristics that you can use to monitor whether you've found a good partner is whether or not you find the relationship to be energy-giving or energy-draining. Does this relationship have that special SPARC?

Think of your relationships with the people you encounter in your work now, either direct colleagues, or persons outside of your organization. Some relationships fill you with energy, motivation, drive, and enthusiasm. Some relationships inspire dread, caution, worry, or exhaustion. And some don't move you toward either end of that energy continuum at all, and leave you flat in the middle.

It's my feeling that for purposes of a strong SPARC partnership, you must seek those partners who give you the feeling of increased energy. In time, as you learn to manage multiple SPARC relationships, you can afford an occasional "energy neutral" partner. For all of us, energy-draining partners will do us no lasting good.

Remember to be self-aware as to the type of energy you bring to your partner, also. If your organization is in an emotional slump, your partner will sense this, and you may find them unwilling to engage with you. Businesses often go through seasonal cycles, almost like mood swings. If your business enjoys predictable highs and lows, I suggest that you remain aware of those cycles, and be honest with your partner. Choose dates for collaborative events where there is likely to be high positive energy.

7 CALL TO ACTION

Good things come to those who... ACT!

It's my hope that by the time you've reached this chapter, you are motivated to take a forward step to grow your small business or strengthen your nonprofit organization, and set an example for others in your community. That means it is time to take action. Here are some things you can do right now to get ready to experience the benefits of SPARC and LIFE.

Call To Action #1: Get your own house in order

If you are a small business owner, you've got some prepping to do before you approach a nonprofit partner. Some first steps are:

Engage your business's key leaders in a conversation about your plans, ask for their input, and get their support. If you are a sole proprietorship, maybe this means talking to your spouse or life partner. If your business is slightly larger, then you talk to the folks who have leadership roles in your business.

Engage your employees in conversation, too. Let them know your desire to build your company's reputation in the community, and give them reason to be enthused and proud to work for you.

Conduct an Assets Inventory to which I referred in Chapter 3. Find the URL in the Appendix, and go to my website where you can order the do-it-yourself reference guide for a nominal cost. Finally, contact me if you'd like me to lead a workshop at your institution where we build your assets inventory together.

If you are a nonprofit director, your list of first actions is similar.

Engage your organization's advisory board or leadership in a conversation about your plans, ask for their input, and get their support.

Engage your volunteers in conversation, too. Let them know your desire to build awareness and support for your nonprofit in the community, and give them reason to be enthused and proud to volunteer for you.

Conduct an Assets Inventory to which I referred in Chapter 3. Find the URL in the Appendix, and go to my website where you can order the do-it-yourself reference guide for a nominal cost. Finally, contact me if you'd like me to lead a workshop at your institution where we build your assets inventory together.

Call To Action #2: Clarify your mission and values

If you don't have a published mission and values statement, don't go any further until you develop them. The SPARC concept relies heavily on this as a discussion point between you and your prospective partners.

The strength of the mission statement comes when it is incorporated into the daily experience of your employees, volunteers, leaders, and advisors. Moreover, if your customers or those whom you serve can feel your mission statement, you have a good indication that the statement is real, and not just a collection of hollow words.

Here's a quick example. I once worked at the Mayo Clinic in Rochester, Minnesota, where the primary value is expressed this way: "The needs of the patient come first." Not a day went by where I was not reminded of this value. Additionally, I could refer to it as a guide when I was faced with a challenging situation in my work. In spite of the fact that I didn't work directly with patients, the primary value statement was so powerful that I was able to apply it confidently in my work.

Call To Action #3: Organize a SPARC workshop in your community

I've seen the most progress in building SPARC relationships when I can actually bring a group of small business owners and nonprofit directors together into one room to engage each other in conversation. We go through the SPARC model together, and engage in initial conversations. As a result, all participants gain direct experience in using the language of SPARC to identify partners who are a good fit, as well as those who are not. Again, the value of this model is that it provides you a reason to say "No" as often as it provides a reason to say "Yes".

I've run a prototypical version of the SPARC workshop in collaboration with my local small business association, with a public school foundation, even with my local professional hockey team, all of which had natural motivations to bring small businesses and nonprofits together for the betterment of the community.

And that's what I would like to do for you and your community. If you are not in a position to host a workshop, notify your local small business association or chamber of commerce and ask them to reach out me. Together we can get the ball rolling in your area.

Let's summarize the key points of the previous chapters.

You are striving for a habit of giving that is **sustainable** from both sides.

You are building a **partnership** that transcends the standard donor-recipient model found in conventional philanthropy.

You have many more **assets** at your disposal to benefit your partner than you may realize, so find them and leverage them.

You are building a **relationship** not just between a small business and a nonprofit, but between the people who work in them.

Since the focus of SPARC is not about giving money, the power of this arrangement comes in the **commitment** you make to your partner.

Furthermore, you add LIFE to the SPARC when you:

Remember to **Laugh**

Work from a position of **Independence**

Seek the right **Fit**

Develop positive **Energy**

8 SUMMARY

A spirit of giving enriches communities.

SPARC is not a quick fix for small business owners who have been in operation for several years but find themselves struggling. Nor is it an immediate recipe for success for the first time startup business owner. Rather, SPARC is a means for small business owners and local nonprofit directors to cut through the polluted economic and political rhetoric of our time and begin the conversation about how to help each other no matter their politics. A spirit of sustainable philanthropy is missing from our national conversation. SPARC provides the language and mechanism to bring a giving spirit into our local communities.

I remind you that SPARC assumes a state of readiness on the part of both the small business owner and the nonprofit leader. My deepest wish is that those of you who are ready to engage in either side of the philanthropic formula describe in these pages will use the SPARC tools to your best advantage.

Further, when you do, I hope you will share your stories with me, and allow me to share them with others who can benefit from your example.

I wish you best success in your endeavors!

Respectfully,

Rick Swanson

9 APPENDICES

Appendix #1 "SPARC a Conversation" Interview Tool

Use the following tool to take notes when you have a SPARC conversation with a potential partner. A downloadable pdf file of this tool is available at:

https://www.rickswanson.com/request-free-guide

Appendix #2

In Chapter 3 I discussed the importance of identifying your organization's assets, for the purposes of strengthening your position as a potential philanthropic partner. Please order a copy of the Assets Inventory Guide at our website for a nominal cost:

https://www.rickswanson.com/product-page/assets-inventory-guide

Remember to update your assets inventory periodically, perhaps annually.

ABOUT THE AUTHOR

Richard P. Swanson is an educator, author, artist, small business advocate, and co-owner of Fox and Swan Arts. Frustrated by conventional models of philanthropy which rely on the exchange of large sums of money, Swanson pulled together disparate elements from the practices of networking, charitable giving, masterminding, process improvement, and business development to create the SPARC tools presented here.

Rick lives in Rochester, Minnesota, with his wife, Janet, and their dog, Macc.

www.ingramcontent.com/pod-product-compliance
Lightning Source LLC
Chambersburg PA
CBHW052229150726
48002CB00003B/1334